Deerfield, IL

www.perrone-ambrose.com

1-800-648-0543

Copyright 2006 © Perrone-Ambrose Associates, Inc.
All rights reserved.

The Mentee's Navigator

Jim Perrone
Larry Ambrose

7th Printing 2009

ISBN 0-9777540-2-2

Foreword

Embarking on a mentoring journey, it will soon become clear that you are committing to becoming more *intentional* about how you learn and grow on the job. You will look at work, your day-to-day assignments, duties, and projects in a new way. You will become the *Navigator* - using your workplace as a living laboratory for accelerated professional growth.

Working with a mentor, you will try to be open to new things. You may make mistakes and do things over. Maybe you'll stumble and fall, but you'll get back up, brush yourself off and start over again.

Your mentor will be with you as your dedicated learning partner. This is the unique aspect of mentoring. It is not unusual to have a manager, a teacher, a parent, a relative, or even a colleague who has been a mentor to you. But it is truly special to have a relationship with another person whose mentoring role with you is the primary reason for the relationship. That very fact focuses and empowers the entire partnership.

Your mentor will be your guide, your partner and colleague, your teacher and your friend. Indeed, as your partnership develops, your mentor will be your fellow learner, deriving benefit and new perspectives from you as well. We hope this book will be an additional companion as a support and as a record of your adventures and progress.

The authors, Jim Perrone and Larry Ambrose, are co-founders of Perrone-Ambrose Associates, Inc., a consulting firm dedicated to improving organizations through the development of their people. Jim and Larry have been innovators in the fields of Mentoring and Coaching for over 20 years, creating the concept of the Strategic Mentoring Support Cycle. The Mentee's Navigator is the latest in a succession of seminal mentoring publications, designed to provide nurture for those engaged in the pursuit of life-long learning.

We wish to gratefully acknowledge all who have contributed to our ongoing discovery of the nuances of mentoring and coaching - our wonderful clients who give us the opportunity to work with their organizations; our staff and consultants who have proved invaluable in pushing the edges of the professional envelope; and those mentors and mentees who have made the decision to engage in partnerships in learning and growth. In particular, we thank Paula Moscinski, who contributed creativity and innovative input to this book. To Noreen Gorman, whose dedication kept us focused on the mission and whose repeated editing contributed to the logic of the book; to Simone Nathan, whose ideas and way with the written word rescued us time and again from the mundane; and to Linda Stockton, who reminds us of our roles as mentors and whose feedback on this book has been invaluable, we say a heartfelt "Thank You."

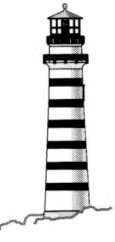

Contents

Page

Forward

Chapter One — 1
The Guiding Principles of Mentee Success

Chapter Two — 15
Creating a Focus for Mentoring

Chapter Three — 23
Building a Partnership with a Mentor

Chapter Four: Periodic Reviews — 37
The "How Am I Doing?" Check-Up Guide
The Success Behaviors Check-Up Guide

Chapter Five — 57
The Mentee's Planner

Conclusion — 75

Appendix — 77
    Additional Focus Exercises
    Finding a Mentor

Chapter 1

The Guiding Principles of Mentee Success

"The future is not some place we are going to but one we are creating. The paths are not to be found, but made, and the activity of making them changes both the maker and the destination."

~ John Schaar,
   University of Santa Clara

The Navigator is your handbook as you prepare for mentoring and as you refine your perspective on professional development.

The planning tools, the awareness-building exercises and the assessment surveys are all here to help you determine the outcomes you hope to gain from working with a mentor. The Appendix contains two supplementary features: additional focus exercises for refining your mentoring aims, and helpful hints on how to find and select a mentor, if you don't already have one.

The Mentee's Navigator is built on these principles of mentee success:

- ◊ Driving your mentoring experience
- ◊ Managing how and what you learn
- ◊ Building on your strengths
- ◊ Surpassing your comfort limits
- ◊ Making your partnership the cornerstone of the mentoring experience

These principles confirm that mentoring is about possibilities, not about fixing problems. Being a mentee is about generating opportunities, not correcting weaknesses; it is about succeeding, not settling.

The goal of the mentoring experience can be quantum leaps, not only incremental improvements. It is more than learning and achieving goals; it is making your life's passion a reality. Successful mentoring reaffirms your sense of direction; it makes you innovative; it erases complacency. Ultimately, the mentoring experience inspires an excitement about your career that captures your *heart as well as your mind.*

Principle: Driving Your Mentoring Experience

It's your career. You're in charge of it. You're the one who keeps it alive and growing. A mentor cannot do it for you. You know what you want from your career and how you can use a mentor's help as you move toward your goals. This means setting goals that you really want to accomplish and being willing to leave your comfort zone. It also means that you, and you alone, will provide the energy and hard work necessary to stay focused on what you want to accomplish.

Principle: *Managing* How and What You Learn

Not only are mentees proactive in driving the mentoring partnership, they actively pursue challenging new learning opportunities. Mentees consistently put themselves into situations that make them stretch their capacity, try out new approaches and broaden their perspective. So, as a mentee, you will be looking at current projects, both successes and mistakes, in terms of what learning you can take away from these experiences. Managing your learning means finding opportunities, projects, and activities that move you along an intentional growth path. It also means being able to identify how all of these opportunities connect to your aspirations for the future. You'll get in the habit of asking yourself, "what did I learn from this?" and "how can I use these lessons of experience as I move forward in my career?"

Principle: *Building* on Your Strengths

Have you taken a clear look at your strengths? It is not unusual to look at oneself and think of all the things that need improvement or change. As a mentee, however, you need to be fully aware of your strengths, talents and abilities. Such awareness enables you to construct a realistic foundation for long-term success. What do you do instinctively well? Awareness of your basic talents helps determine the paths you might follow to steer through blind alleys and dead ends. Insight into your capacities helps you push yourself into situations where you will have the best chance of succeeding, and gives you the optimistic energy to pursue the right challenges. Finally, when you understand and respect your strengths and confidently share them with your mentor, you help him or her know how to best work with you.

Principle: *Surpassing* Your Comfort Limits

Becoming a mentee, by definition, means that you expect to think in some new ways, try new things, explore new avenues. As a mentee, you will be asked by your mentor to challenge yourself, to live outside of your comfort zone, and to not settle for being average. You'll try to think and act "bigger," to test your resolve and your commitment to excel. Having a "surpass your limits orientation" means concentrating on being great, not just good enough. Willingness to surpass your comfort limits guarantees that you'll be open to your mentor's challenging your view of what is possible, pushing you to do it just a bit better, and asking you to stretch toward your next horizon.

Principle: *Making Your Partnership the Cornerstone*

Every successful mentoring partnership is a collaboration, co-created by the mentee and the mentor. Your partnership will be like no other. Your partnership needs to live up to no one's expectations except those of the two of you. Your pairing is a unique opportunity for you to pursue your own goals using the tailored assistance of a caring and committed mentoring partner. The formation and nurturing of your partnership is critically important, and the responsibility rests on both of you. Everything turns on the quality of your partnership. This requires that you determine what you most want from your mentor. It requires that your mentor returns your efforts with a strong dedication to meet your needs.

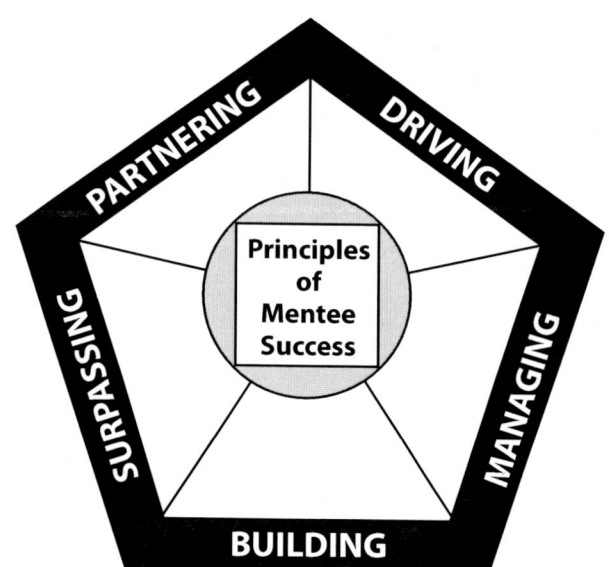

About Mentoring - What kind of people are mentees?

Mentees are people who want to learn and grow and who desire to take charge of their own careers. They believe the learning journey will be greatly enhanced if accompanied by a trusted guide. In a fishing expedition, the guide points out the shallows and the speed of the current, but does not bring in the fish. That is the fisher's job. It is the same in a mentoring partnership. The mentor, familiar with the territory, may assist in the navigation, but the mentee accepts the challenge to steer the course and to achieve the tangible outcomes made possible by their collaboration.

The mentor helps the mentee to develop an eye for opportunity, and aids in seeing possibilities. Responding to the mentor, the mentee notices growth opportunities in the everyday events of the job and builds the drive and ability to take advantage of them. Creative mentees see how opportunities contribute to their long-term benefit and how working with an experienced mentor can provide energy, wisdom and exposure to new perspectives and points of view. Successful mentees are self-starters, aware of both their strengths and their needs, who take full responsibility for their professional success.

As you begin your time as a mentee, it will be valuable for you to consider how you rate yourself on a number of competencies that support effective mentees. For example, it will be helpful to gain insight about those aspects of mentee behavior that will be easy for you, and those that will be challenging. The Mentee Self-Assessment on the following pages will help you gain insight about yourself at the inception of the mentoring experience and will assist you in working as a full partner with your mentor.

The Mentee Self-Assessment

The Mentee Self-Assessment will help you consider how well you use opportunities for growth and learning.

Give yourself a rating from 1 to 6 on the following items for how closely each statement describes your learning behavior (6 for very closely; 1 for not closely at all):

How receptive are you to new learning?

Receptive learners initiate discussions that result in assistance and feedback and are willing to risk being vulnerable in order to reach their full potential.

1. I value and seek feedback from my mentors, my supervisors and my peers even when it is difficult to accept.

                                                                                   1   2   3   4   5   6

   _____

2. I freely share information with my mentor about my struggles and difficulties.

                                                                                   1   2   3   4   5   6

   _____

3. I readily apply the learnings and feedback I receive from others.

                                                                                   1   2   3   4   5   6

   _____

Do you manage your own learning?

Self-managers take the actions and steps necessary to get to the next level in their careers, rather than expecting their mentors to do it for them.

4. I know what I want from my career and I have a professional development plan with objectives and actions.

                                                  1 2 3 4 5 6

                                                  _____

5. I take full responsibility for the success of my relationship with my mentor.

                                                  1 2 3 4 5 6

                                                  _____

6. I seek out new opportunities to gain the additional experience, advice and guidance I need.

                                                  1 2 3 4 5 6

                                                  _____

What is your self-awareness IQ?

Learners with high self-awareness IQs reflect on their own developmental needs and are able to listen to themselves as they react to the people and environment around them.

7. At the end of the day, I reflect on my performance and the events that took place in order to seek new learning.

                                                  1 2 3 4 5 6

                                                  _____

8. I pay conscious attention to how events and situations are affecting my behavior and me.

        1   2   3   4   5   6

        _____

9. I admit it when I make a wrong decision or when my lack of experience gets in the way.

        1   2   3   4   5   6

        _____

Where do you stand on resilience?

Resilient people are willing to be and stay uncomfortable, and initiate and sustain difficult relationships for the sake of growth and learning.

10. I respond to disappointment or setbacks by learning more about what went wrong and how I can do things differently.

        1   2   3   4   5   6

        _____

11. I push myself to do the things I fear in order to attain growth and development.

        1   2   3   4   5   6

        _____

12. I make an effort to take on work and situations that challenge my developmental needs.

        1   2   3   4   5   6

        _____

How growth-oriented are you?

Growth-oriented people actively contribute, take ownership for improving work, and gather feedback in order to become more successful.

13. When opinions differ or disagreements occur, I try to understand why someone else's view is different from mine.

                                                 1 2 3 4 5 6

   _____

14. I look to see how much I can learn instead of how often I can be right.

                                                 1 2 3 4 5 6

   _____

15. I proactively initiate learning, versus reacting to daily tasks.

                                                 1 2 3 4 5 6

   _____

How well do you learn at a double-loop level?

Self-learners are those who, in the solving of one problem, learn something about preventing similar problems.

16. I explore how my way of thinking about a problem may be getting in the way of solving it.

                                                 1 2 3 4 5 6

   _____

17. I pay attention to my patterns of behavior and how they impact my effectiveness.

                                        1   2   3   4   5   6

                                        _____

18. I identify solutions that prevent problems from recurring.

                                        1   2   3   4   5   6

                                        _____

Mentee Competencies:

The Self-Assessment examines six major "Mentee Competency Areas". Each of the six boxes above concentrated on one of these competencies. They are explained below, followed by some worksheets for additional analysis.

Receptivity

People committed to improvement and learning signal their openness to new information, approaches and ideas. They are willing to self-disclose, ask for help, solicit new ideas and try new ways of doing things. They actively seek input and feedback from others even when the information may make them uncomfortable.

Self-Management

Successful mentees take responsibility for their career decisions and for the actions they can take to ensure the desired progress. They know they must drive the mentoring relationship, keep it moving and sustain the energy to keep it alive.

Self-Awareness

Mentees get the most out of mentoring by recognizing their own strengths and weaknesses and studying how their actions impact others. By acknowledging what they do well and what they must improve, they demonstrate a sense of personal confidence and honesty.

Growth Orientation

Those who get the most from a mentoring experience have a deep-set investment in personal improvement. They develop a clear agenda for where they are going and what they need to do to get there.

Resilience

Successful career learners realize that the key to success is not in doing everything perfectly the first time, but in having the strength to make mistakes, stumble, sometimes fall, then rise for another try. They see each stumble as a potential step toward their ultimate vision of success. . . and they deliberately examine the learning they get from the experience.

Double-Loop Learning Focus

Mentees need to learn at a deeper level, by examining trends and root causes of problems (double-loop learning), rather then just dealing with symptoms and superficial approaches to problems (single loop learning). They are willing to examine how their actions, habits and ways of thinking may contribute to problems and how these habits may hamper further professional growth.

Now that you have completed the checklist, go over it again and select two of the behaviors from the total group of eighteen that are most important for you to stress:

List the behaviors below and what you can do to improve in those areas:
1._____
_____
_____
_____

2._____
_____
_____
_____

In the next chapter you will have the opportunity to do some organized reflection on your professional growth goals. But before doing specific work on your goals, ask yourself the following questions. Answer the questions instinctively instead of trying to come up with a "right" answer.

1. What's in it for me to become more intentional and focused on how I learn on the job?
_____
_____
_____

2. What makes this a good time to get really serious about the progress I desire in my career?
_____
_____
_____

3. What are some non-negotiable outcomes that I am committed to achieving as a result of this mentoring year?

_____
_____
_____

4. What excites me most about having a mentoring opportunity?

_____
_____
_____

5. What, if anything, is threatening about this?

_____
_____
_____

6. How might I get in the way of making mentoring a great experience?

_____
_____
_____

After reviewing your responses, what is your impression of your readiness to begin a mentoring journey? (Rate your readiness on a scale of 1 to 10)

Readiness Score:

No, Not Ready   Later, Not Yet   Pretty Soon   Ready Now

1   2   3   4   5   6   7   8   9   10

This is what I can do to increase my readiness score.

_____
_____
_____

A Speech on the Occasion of My Retirement

Imagine that you are about to attend your retirement celebration. It is common that speeches are given on these occasions. If you could compose the speech you would like to hear someone deliver about your career, what would you include? How do you want your career to be described by your colleagues and managers at the time of your retirement? What personal and professional characteristics would you like to hear highlighted? What accomplishments would you like your presenter to catalogue? Use the space below to compose that ideal retirement speech.

_____
_____
_____
_____
_____
_____
_____
_____
_____
_____
_____
_____

Chapter Two will concentrate on getting specific about a focus for your mentoring experience. As you go through the steps of creating a focus for mentoring, think back to the reflections you've completed in Chapter One.

Chapter 2

Creating a Focus for Mentoring

"I've never made a mistake.
I've only learned from experience."

~ Thomas A. Edison

What do we mean by *"a focus for mentoring?"* A mentoring focus can be anything you want it to be, whether it is: gaining more knowledge about your organization; acquiring or polishing a particular skill; or deciding upon your next career move. Focus is merely getting clear about the results you want from your mentoring experience.

This chapter contains a number of activities designed to help you reflect and take stock of your aspirations and the areas you are targeting for professional growth:

1. Reviewing your experience and the strengths you bring to a mentoring partnership.
2. Deciding what you want from your mentoring relationship.
3. Defining your professional growth goals.

1. Reviewing

To begin, consider the questions below to review your past experience and to experiment with the prospect of working with a mentor:

What have been some of the most important developmental experiences in your career?

_____
_____
_____
_____

How would you describe your contribution to the organization? What would you like it to be in the future?

_____
_____
_____
_____

How would your manager and colleagues describe you, your skills and style? How would you like them to describe you a year from now?

_____
_____
_____
_____

What are you passionate about in your career? What in your job holds your attention and involves your imagination?

_____
_____
_____
_____

What do you find most challenging for you? What behavior, or skill, do you most resist tackling?

_____
_____
_____
_____

List your top five strengths.

_____
_____
_____
_____

2. Deciding what you want

The core purpose of this chapter is to produce clear professional growth goals to guide your mentoring partnership. List the qualities, behaviors and practices that you want to be a part of the relationship with your mentor. Then identify the expectations that you have for yourself and your mentor - expectations that will help cultivate the mentoring relationship you want.

Your ideal mentoring relationship: If it's working great, what would the relationship look like?

_____
_____
_____

Your expectations of yourself:

_____
_____
_____

What should you begin doing, or do more of?

_____
_____
_____

What should you stop doing, or do less of?

_____
_____
_____

What do you need your mentor to challenge you on?

_____
_____
_____

What do you need your mentor to support you by doing?

_____
_____
_____

3. Defining your professional growth goals

Look at your responses on the previous checklists: **Reviewing,** on page 16; and **Deciding** what you want on page 17. Use your answers to the questions on these worksheets to begin defining your professional growth goals. **Additional Focus Exercises are provided in the Appendix, pages 78-81 to aid you in refining your needs and aspirations further.

Setting goals

View your mentoring experience as an opportunity to get one step closer to your career vision. Professional growth goals give your mentoring experience purpose, direction and focus. Growth goals are derived from identifying your "growth edge." *A growth edge is that behavior, skill, or personal characteristic that you resist attending to or dealing with. However, given the appropriate energy and attention, identifying and working on your growth edge can help you to be more productive and feel more personally fulfilled.*

What do you believe to be your growth edge?

_____
_____
_____
_____
_____

What, if anything, keeps you from confronting and working with your growth edge?

_____
_____
_____
_____
_____

The following steps outline the process for creating your professional growth goals.

Step 1: Formulate growth edge statements
Express your growth edge in clear action terms.

> Example of a growth edge statement: *"To be more detail oriented in planning and implementing projects".*

My growth edge statement:

_____
_____
_____
_____
_____

Step 2: Determine the outcome you want
Ask yourself what you want to achieve by dealing with your growth edge.

> Building on the example above: *"Avoiding errors of oversight that cause less than excellent results in project management."*

Statements of my desired outcomes:

_____
_____
_____
_____

Step 3: Write a professional growth goal
Prepare a goal statement in terms of observable outcomes:

<u>Example of a professional growth goal statement:</u> *"Insure excellent, error-free project management by a heightened attention to detail."*

Professional growth goal statement:

_____
_____
_____

Having completed the steps outlined above, you now have a mentoring focus, one that will guide both you and your mentor in getting started on your partnership.

With that focus firmly in hand, you can begin building your mentoring partnership in Chapter Three.

Chapter 3

Building a Partnership With a Mentor

When the explorer is ready,
The guide will appear.

~ Himalayan proverb

The ancient Himalayan saying offers real truth. You will make best use of a mentor *only when you are ready to apply important lessons.* The mentor may offer help, but if you are not ready or are not prepared to take responsibility for your own professional development, the help will be of no consequence.

We asked a group of mentors what they enjoyed most about mentoring. One mentor's response captured the essence:

"Helping someone figure out the next step. I never had an objective person to do that for me in my career."

Your mentor is a person who wants you to achieve your personal and professional best. It is your mentor's job to provide support and encouragement, while still challenging you to strive to reach your potential. Mentors do not let mentees be comfortable with being just OK, or "staying small."

Ask someone who has worked with a mentor:

> "My mentor lends new perspectives to various situations. It's really nice to get an overview and a personal perspective from someone at the level she's at. Having a mentor with her resources and approach is a new opportunity for me. And she has a fresh view on things. It's been eye-opening."

Mentoring partnerships exist solely to make mentoring happen; there is no other reason. Mentoring exists to help you take full advantage of learning and growth possibilities. You will build the mentoring partnership as the means for stretching and surpassing your limits.

Building a mentoring partnership requires that both mentor and mentee take a planned approach to building their relationship. This includes:
- Clarifying expectations of each other and the roles you will fulfill
- Getting to know each other as persons
- Sharing and agreeing on expectations of the experience itself

By virtue of great experience or simply by their relative distance from your immediate situation, mentors can help in a myriad of ways.

> **What will you get from a mentor that you wouldn't get working by yourself on your professional development?**
>
> *The benefit of hearing a different point of view; the opportunity to think out loud and test your ideas with a partner; having your very own devil's advocate; receiving suggestions from an experienced person devoted to your enhancement; being challenged in ways you wouldn't challenge yourself.*

Your mentoring partnership

Linking-Up with a Mentor and Sustaining a Partnership

Just what does an effective mentoring partnership look like? All successful mentoring partnerships share some common characteristics:

- Clear understanding and agreement about what each partner will do in the relationship
- Unambiguous mutual commitment by both partners to each other and to the partnership itself
- Shared responsibility for the success of the partnership
- Candid honesty in communication and feedback between mentor and mentee

It is vitally important that you and your mentor have a formal "Link-Up" meeting to set up your relationship. The purpose is to make sure that each of you has defined your expectations as you begin the partnership. The Link-Up is the time to formally introduce yourself and your goals to your mentor in a thorough discussion. Such a discussion gives both of you the opportunity to explore each other's ideas, needs, and goals, and to find out what you expect of each other.

Prior to linking-up

Give your mentor the **"To my mentor"** sheet on page 26, ask him or her to fill it out and be ready to discuss responses with you at the meeting. Also complete the **"Notes to myself"** page 28 and discuss your reactions at the meeting. Talking over these questions will help kick-start the getting-acquainted process.

To my mentor:

We are about to begin what I hope will be a fulfilling and mutually satisfying experience for both of us. We'll be having our first meeting soon. Please take a few minutes to review these questions before we meet. I will be completing a similar worksheet on myself as well. We can share our responses at our first get-together.

1. What do you expect from me as your mentee?

2. What do you feel most able to help me with?

3. How do you prefer to work with people you are teaching and developing?

4. What are you personally seeking to gain from a mentoring relationships with a mentee?

Review each of your professional growth goals (page 21) before the Link-Up meeting and ask yourself questions about each:

What's the challenge in this goal? What will I have to change about myself in order to achieve this goal? How can my mentor help me achieve this? How might I hinder myself from achieving this goal? What will I gain from its accomplishment?

Having prepared your professional growth goals and completed your "**Notes to myself,**" (page 28) it's time to get together for your Link-Up Meeting.

Notes to myself:

While your mentor is preparing for the Link-Up meeting, review and be ready with responses to the questions below:

1. What about me will contribute to my being a successful mentee?

2. What about me could get in the way or hinder my taking maximum advantage of this mentoring year?

3. What does success look like for me?
   I'll know I've succeeded when . . .

The Link-Up Meeting

Your Link-Up meeting initiates the "sizing-up" process, looking each other over. Approach the link-up with open minds, clear goals and specific expectations.

Both you and your mentor can view the mentoring partnership as a key career opportunity. The best mentors are also learners, always seeking to learn more and gain new perspectives from their mentees. The Link-Up meeting may be the most important single meeting of your mentorship. So it's worth doing right and worth preparing for.

This meeting will give your relationship direction. Make sure to emphasize your hope that scheduled meetings will not be the only time you communicate with each other. Before your meeting is over, decide on when you will next meet.

When you meet for Link-Up, bring your professional growth goals from page 21. Your mentor will be ready to hear you review and discuss these goals and to help with alternatives and new ideas.

The "Mentor/Mentee Link-Up Agreement," beginning on the next page, is a good guide for your meeting. Go through the Link-Up Agreement together, item-by-item, and discuss each thoroughly. When you're through and have reached agreement on the elements of the agreement, fill it in and make a copy for your mentor. The Link-Up Agreement will provide structure for your partnership planning and act as a touchstone for reference and review during updates over the course of the year.

Mentor/Mentee Link-Up Agreement

Mentee: _____

Mentor: _____

1. Important information about ourselves that we have shared.

2. Our agreed-upon expectations for the mentoring relationship.

3. The mentee's professional growth goals.

4. The initial growth goal with which to begin work.

5. Some first steps to take toward this goal.

Link-Up Agreement *Continued*

6. Our commitments to make this partnership work.

7. Signs that will show the partnership is working.

8. Items to keep confidential.

Logistics:

Term of the partnership:
_____

Meeting frequency: _____

Our next session will be (date): _____

Preferred method of contact:

☐ Phone ☐ Voice Mail ☐ E-Mail ☐ Admin Asst

Link-Up Agreement *Continued*

Approximate amount of time to be committed by the Mentor per month:

_____

Approximate amount of time to be invested by the Mentee per month:

_____

Additional Expectations and/or Agreements:

_____
_____
_____
_____

We will keep the mentee's supervisor appropriately informed, if applicable.

Mentee: _____   **Mentor:** _____

Date: _____   **Date:** _____

Link-Up Agreement *Continued*

Sustaining a partnership: maintaining contact

Your readiness for the mentoring partnership is signaled by how proactively you reach out to your mentor.

- ❖ Contact your mentor at least once a month, either in person, by phone or email.

- ❖ Don't worry about being a pest; a good mentor will never see you as a pest. Frequent contact and authentic conversation enables you to achieve great clarity and candor in your relationship.

- ❖ Actively solicit feedback from your mentor. Be especially open and non-defensive when you hear your mentor's impressions of your words and behavior.

- ❖ Work to become as introspective as possible; ask your mentor about your impact on others.

- ❖ Work up the courage to give your mentor feedback about how he or she can help you best. What can your mentor do more of, or less of to better aid you?

- ❖ Revisit your growth goals (pages 27) periodically, and set new directions as you achieve initial targets.

- ❖ Let your mentor know your aims and how you feel you are progressing. Your mentor bears a responsibility in your partnership - to be responsive to your needs. So your needs must be made known - whether they are big picture goals or individual issues for which you need only a quick reaction.

Handling your mentoring meetings: the 3-step meeting model

Each time you and your mentor meet - in person or by telephone - it is important that you have some structure for your meetings. Using the 3-Step Meeting Model every time you meet gives your interactions a common-sense structure and helps both of you assess the impact of your efforts.

Step 1: Review Your Progress
Summarize your last assignment or planned activity in the following contexts:
- Your part in the activity.
- Successes and 'wins'. (A 'win' refers to something new that you tried; something you were able to accomplish; or some fear you had in the past, but have overcome.)
- Challenges that you still experience.
- Surprises you have encountered.

Step 2: Review Your Learning
- What worked well?
- What would you do differently next time?
- What changes would you make as a result of your challenge(s)?
- What can you do on your own?
- How can your mentor help?

Step 3: Agree on the Next Steps for You
- Come out of the meeting with a plan.
- Co-create the next opportunity or activity. Brainstorm with your mentor.
- Clarify specific action steps you will complete.
- Set the time and date for your next meeting.

Note: You may wish to record notes from your meetings in the Mentee Planner in Chapter Five.

Periodic review

Review the state of your partnership periodically. It's best to meet about every three months *solely to check on how the partnership is going*. Check-up meetings will review how you are both doing - as mentee and mentor.

Check-ups allow you to stand back and assess how far you've come in creating your relationship. You have made personal observations about what is working and not working. You have, most likely, noted how well you've worked together. These reviews allow you to revisit and refresh your mission together. You might decide on one or more of these in your review:

- Re-visit and clarify your original goals.
- Pare down the number of goals.
- Revise or create new growth goals.
- Affirm or redirect the course of your mentoring experience.
- Identify actions you can take to get the most from your mentoring experience.
- Offer suggestions to your mentor about how he or she can best support your learning.

Chapter 4

Periodic Reviews

"Observe perpetually."

~ Henry James

Mentoring partnerships, like all other relationships, have a number of predictable stages through which they progress. The first of these is the "honeymoon" - when both partners feel optimistic and appreciative of each other. But we all know that honeymoons don't last, reality sets in, and the relationship sometimes looks and feels very different than expected. Partnerships can suffer from uncertainty and possibly discouragement at this point. To keep the mentoring partnership fresh and the communication active and open, it is essential that you see your mentoring year as one of carefully maintaining conscious efforts to sustain the relationship. Therefore, periodic review "check-up meetings" between you and your mentor are very important.

Check-Up Guides

Below are two outlines for assessing your contribution to the mentoring partnership and for looking at what you can do to maximize mentoring benefits. These guides, the *"How Am I Doing?" Check-Up* and the *Success Behavior Check-Up* are designed to help you reflect on your mentoring experience as you are going through it.

You might choose to use only one of the assessments, or to use both of them at different junctures in your mentoring relationship. However, we do recommend that you use one of the check-ups 3 to 4 months into your partnership, and the other at the 6 to 7 month point.

The "How Am I Doing?" Check-Up Guide

As a mentee, you have devoted time and commitment to your mentoring partnership. We know of no better way to support your own development than by collaborating with a good mentor.

Periodic reassessment of how you are doing **as a partner with your mentor** is the best way to ensure that the mentorship is kept alive. Experience has shown that regular meetings scheduled **solely to review how you're doing** are fundamental to mentoring success.

How Am I Doing?
Review the descriptive statement(s) below taken from the Self-Assessment on pages 6-10. Reflect on your behavior as a mentee over the months of your mentoring experience and decide if you are dong' "OK" or "Not OK" on each of the items. If you determine that you are doing "Not OK," consider the italicized recommendation following the statement.

1. I know what I want from my career and I have a professional development plan with objectives and actions. (Page 7)

☐ OK
☐ Not OK

If you have individual development plans in your organization, review your plan for reference and explore how you can expand and clarify its meaning for you career. Solicit assistance from your mentor in clarifying what you want and broadening your professional development plan. Your mentor can be viewed as a major resource for ongoing review and updating of your development plans and objectives.

2. At the end of the day, I reflect on my performance and the events that took place, in order to seek new learning. (Page 7)

☐ OK
☐ Not OK

Practice developing the habit of reviewing the major events or activities of each day. Identify what stood out for you. Assign a rating of 1 to 5 for each of these major activities in terms of your performance and what each has taught you.

3. I pay conscious attention to how events and situations are affecting my behavior and me. (Page 8)

☐ OK
☐ Not OK

Reflect on how one significant event or experience has affected you. In addition, solicit feedback from your peers, family and/or supervisor on how they see the effects of such situations on your behavior.

4. I admit it when I make a wrong decision or when my lack of experience gets in the way. (Page 8)

☐ OK
☐ Not OK

You may not be the best judge of this. Solicit feedback from those acquainted with your performance and behavior about how you react when experiencing these difficulties. Ask sincerely for this feedback and remain open to hearing others' honest observations. Also, ask yourself what the cost to yourself and others is in not admitting a wrong decision.

5. I respond to disappointment or setbacks by learning more about what went wrong and how I can do things differently. (Page 8)

☐ OK
☐ Not OK

Reflect on a recent disappointment. What proportion of the setback was your own doing or responsibility? How did you respond at the time? What might you have done differently then? What would you do differently now? Solicit feedback from an individual who was present and witnessed the event.

6. I push myself to do the things I fear in order to attain growth and learning. (Page 8)

☐ OK

☐ Not OK

Reflect and identify factors in a new challenge that make you feel uncomfortable. What factors do you find attractive in a new challenge? When facing your next challenge, identify the forces inherent in that challenge that will advance your learning and growth. Then identify the forces in the challenge that increase your discomfort. Work to increase your appreciation of the forces for learning and growth so that they outweigh the discomforts.

7. I explore how my way of thinking about a problem may be getting in the way of solving it. (Page 9)

☐ OK

☐ Not OK

Break down your approach to thinking through problems. Share the steps with your mentor and pinpoint what in the process might create bottlenecks in your thinking. Identify alternative approaches and choose one with which you will experiment over a period of time.

8. I pay attention to my patterns of behavior and how they impact my effectiveness. (Page 10)

☐ OK

☐ Not OK

Develop a periodic exercise for yourself to develop awareness of how your behavior influences your effectiveness. Pay attention to the nonverbal signals of others as you interact in stress situations. Reflect on how your supervisor reacts to how you present suggestions and proposals. Record your "take" on these observations. Tell your supervisor and associates that you are working on this awareness. Solicit their help in flagging which patterns of your behavior they find helpful and not helpful.

9. I identify solutions that prevent problems from recurring. (Page 10) ☐ OK

☐ Not OK

Ask not only what will solve a current problem you are confronting, but also what you can do to monitor its staying solved. Ask yourself what will tell you that the problem is remaining solved. Also ask what you will look for as early warning signals that the problem may be recurring. If you were teaching someone how to make sure that this problem stays solved, what would you tell them?

My Action Plan:

1. Review your assessment. Select the three most important behaviors for you to focus on during the next two months.

_____
_____
_____

2. List the actions you will take to improve in each behavior.

_____
_____
_____

Now it is time to meet with your mentor for a *"How Am I Doing?"* Check-Up Meeting and share your assessment.

"How Am I Doing?" Check-Up Meeting

The "How Am I Doing?" Check-Up Meeting with your mentor provides you both the opportunity to share how the experience is going and to plan how the partnership can ideally proceed. You may agree to remain on the same track; you may decide to alter course. Your decisions will be based on an open, honest exchange of feedback and reflection. This meeting is for the sole purpose of reviewing your partnership, **not for**

discussion of the mentee's current issues or projects. Conducting such a meeting is an excellent way to ensure that your partnership continues to be fresh and vital through honest feedback shared with each other. Following the Check-Up Meeting, record the agreements below.

Check-Up Meeting Format:

Mentee's action steps:

Mentee's commitments going forward:

Mentor's commitments for the partnership:

_____
_____
_____
_____
_____
_____
_____
_____
_____
_____
_____

Success Behavior Check-Up Guide

This review is designed to assist you and your mentor in looking at what you both see as possible after having devoted several months to mentoring. By using this tool you can take stock of your joint perceptions of the partnership and conduct a Success Behavior Check-Up Meeting to plan your own focus and that of your mentor.

You may find that you have achieved the professional development objectives set at the beginning of the partnership. Along the way you or your mentor may have discovered patterns of behavior that remain as challenges. You may have noticed behaviors with which you have not yet experimented. You both may see ways in which your partnership can be retooled to be more beneficial to both of you as you progress through your mentoring partnership.

The most effective way to use this tool is for you and your mentor to meet together to discuss your individual impressions.

Progress Review:

How has your mentoring partnership evolved since it began?

_____
_____
_____
_____
_____
_____
_____
_____
_____
_____

How would a non-biased person view your mentoring partnership?

_____
_____
_____
_____
_____
_____
_____
_____
_____
_____

Success Behavior Areas

Below are five style descriptions for Success Behavior, each has special significance to your professional development and success. You may find one or more of these areas of behavior very natural to your overall style and manner, while other areas pose a great challenge. It is common for an individual to be effective in some, but not all, of these preferred patterns of behavior. A systematic assessment of the behavioral areas that present a challenge to your overall skill and style will help set an agenda for broadening and balancing your overall professional development. Review the definitions below and complete a self-assessment (pages 47-51) in those stretch/challenge areas that could benefit from your additional concentration.

Assertion/Risk Taking: Is oriented toward action and results. Accepts challenge. Makes decisions quickly. Takes on authority. Manages trouble. Solves problems.

Outreach/Influencing: Prefers to communicate through talking. Creates a motivating environment. Welcomes possibilities. Takes initiative in relationships and contact. Generates enthusiasm.

Organization/Self-Management: Focuses on the actual and the concrete. Performs and behaves in a consistent manner. Creates a stable, harmonious work environment. Uses cause and effect thinking. Strives for objective thinking and results. Analyzes performance by weighing costs and benefits.

Openness/Supporting: Attunes to the external and to relationships. Works effectively in group settings. Exhibits loyalty and demonstrates patience. Creates a non-threatening managerial environment. Provides help to others.

Innovation/Creativity: Uses imagination in making decisions. Focuses on how facts relate and connect. Concentrates on the big picture and on abstract reasoning. Pays attention to patterns of behavior. Recognizes new opportunities. Thinks "outside the box."

My Success Behavior Assessment

Review each of the five Success Behavior assessment boxes below. Which of the success behavior areas remain challenges for your professional growth? Which of these areas do you tend to avoid or ignore? Having checked one or more of the boxes, review the menu of actions in the box to stimulate your thinking about steps you might take to build strength in that success behavior. If any of the actions on the menu is one you need to attempt, place an "X" in the space next to it. If none of the actions is specifically relevant for you, use the spaces below the menu to compose some action steps you may take to improve in the particular area. Solicit suggestions from your mentor during your Check-Up Meeting.

Check to Select Area: ☐	**Assertion/Risk Taking: Oriented toward action and results. Accepts challenge. Makes decisions quickly. Takes on authority. Manages trouble. Solves problems.**
	Do your homework, formulate a plan and enthusiastically pursue your proposal.
	Complete a project with a tight deadline.
	Take a tough-minded stance and hold firm.
	Take on a difficult project (last person failed).
	Make peace with an enemy.
	Experiment with making decisions more quickly, even if you do not have all the desired data.

Other Action Steps:

Check to Select Area: ☐	**Innovation/Creativity: Uses imagination in making decisions. Focuses on how facts relate and connect. Concentrates on the big picture and on abstract reasoning. Pays attention to patterns of behavior relationships. Recognizes new opportunities. Thinks "outside the box."**
	Write a proposal for a new trend/technique; present to others in a group.
	Study creative thinking techniques.
	In solving a problem, think of several options besides the one you think is correct. Challenge your original assumptions.
	Do an executive summary describing the trends the data suggests.
	Sit in a meeting of one of the creative functions in the organization. How can you use that group's thought or problem solving processes in your work?
	Take a literature, art or music appreciation course. Learn to look for subtle meanings: What is this book really about? What does this song mean? What hidden message would the customer/direct report/student get from this?

Other Action Steps:

Check to Select Area: ☐	**Openness/Supporting:** Attunes to the external and to relationships. Works effectively in group settings. Exhibits loyalty and demonstrates patience. Creates a non-threatening managerial environment. Provides help to others.
	Find ways to be appreciative of others. Keep track of your ratio of compliments to criticism.
	Open up with a trusted person and share what you are thinking.
	If you think someone might be of help, ask for assistance, especially if you prefer to go it alone.
	Practice holding your tongue for periods of time in meetings, especially if you are in charge.
	Mentor a young person.
	Give someone simple, to-the-point feedback.

Other Action Steps:

Check to Select Area: ☐	**Organization/Self-Management: Focuses on the actual and the concrete. Performs and behaves in a consistent manner. Creates a stable, harmonious work environment. Uses cause and effect thinking. Strives for objective thinking and results. Analyzes performance by weighing costs.**
	Use precise, accurate details in written and spoken communications, even though you may think it is not necessary.
	Slow down in your actions. Ask yourself, "Have I given enough thought to this?"
	Do a problem prevention analysis.
	Focus on reality in its most concrete form — data, resources, physical characteristics, etc.
	Speak in direct and specific terms.
	Practice completing less-important tasks a day or two before the deadline instead of letting them wait until the last minute because they are less important.

Other Action Steps:

Check to Select Area: ☐	**Outreach/Influencing: Prefers to communicate through talking. Creates a motivating environment. Welcomes possibilities. Takes initiative in relationships and contacts. Generates enthusiasm.**
	Speak up in meetings when you feel enthusiastic about a point of view.
	Have lunch with one new business contact per week — increase your networking circle.
	Become active in a professional organization.
	Find ways to gain cooperation rather than compliance. "What's in it for other people if they join with me?"
	Seek the opportunity to work on a task force to solve a problem or plan a new project.
	Once a week take an action spontaneously. Reflect on how the situation worked out and how it felt.

Other Action Steps:

Gains from Mentoring:

My gains from the mentoring experience:

_____
_____
_____
_____
_____
_____
_____
_____
_____
_____
_____

If you stopped your mentoring relationship now, what would not have been accomplished? What would have been left unfinished or untried?

_____
_____
_____
_____
_____
_____
_____
_____
_____
_____
_____

Going Forward

Some mentoring partnerships are very active, with a close bond having been formed, and many goals completed. Not all partnerships fit this description. Some pairs are not so active. Time, events, geography, travel and assignments often complicate the most positive of intentions. You may not have accomplished all you had wished for your partnership. That's still OK. It's what you do from here on that is most important. There's still plenty of time.

What is one tangible thing outside your comfort zone - something you don't do well or naturally - that you can work on to get the most out of mentoring? (Behavior patterns, thought processes, initiatives.)

In order to maximize the benefits of the mentoring experience for you, what could your mentor:
    Do More of or Begin Doing?

_____
_____
_____

    Do Less of or Stop Doing?

_____
_____
_____

    Continue Doing?

_____
_____
_____

Now it is time to meet with your mentor for a Success Behavior Check-Up Meeting and share your assessment.

Success Behavior Check-Up Meeting

The Success Behavior Check-Up meeting with your mentor provides you both the opportunity to share your impressions and plan how you will continue to use this experience. You may agree to remain on the same track; you may plan certain changes. Your decisions will be based on an open, honest exchange of feedback and reflection. This meeting is for the sole purpose of reviewing your partnership, **not for discussion of the mentee's current issues or projects.** Conducting such a meeting is an excellent way to ensure that your partnership remains fresh and vital.

Success Behavior Meeting format:

Mentee's action steps

_____
_____
_____
_____
_____
_____
_____

Mentee's commitments to the partnership

_____
_____
_____
_____
_____
_____
_____
_____

Mentor's commitments to the partnership

_____
_____
_____
_____
_____
_____
_____
_____

Chapter 5

The Mentee's Planner

"We are what we perpetually do.
Excellence, then, is not an act but a habit."

~ Aristotle

Working with a mentor in a mentoring partnership is all about learning and trying new things. Mentees learn from a range of sources: advice and coaching from a mentor; observing role models; experimenting with new methods; seeking new and sometimes daunting new challenges; attempting and failing at unfamiliar tasks. Learning involves courage and resilience, and the willingness to put oneself into uncomfortable circumstances for the sake of building new capacity. Also essential to learning is the process of organized reflection and drawing conclusions from that reflection. Learning also involves change or the willingness to change. And change cannot result without planning new actions for the future.

The Mentee's Planner is provided for the purposes outlined above. It has four sections:
1. **Successes and Wins** - those activities in which you have attempted new behavior and have experienced positive outcomes.
2. **Challenges** - those activities you've attempted that remain unfinished, have been less than successful or present ongoing challenges for you.
3. **Action Plans** - activities, assignments, projects or new approaches that you can work on to achieve your development goals.
4. **Information to Share with My Mentor** - issues of success or challenge that you can discuss with your mentor; new learning that is important to you; or specific feedback you should give to your mentor concerning your partnership, its progress or character.

The Mentee's Planner is to be used to keep you and your mentor current in your mentoring experience. It acts as your ongoing "journal" or "diary" of the mentoring year. Most of all, it serves as a major planning and goal-setting source to ensure that your mentoring partnership produces the results you seek. You'll find a column heading for "Date" on the diary pages. It is there for your convenience if you desire to record the date of your notes.

Successes and Wins - activities in which I have attempted new behavior successfully.

Date	Activity or Behavior and What I have learned

Successes and Wins - activities in which I have attempted new behavior successfully.

Date	Activity or Behavior and What I have learned

Successes and Wins - activities in which I have attempted new behavior successfully.

Date	Activity or Behavior and What I have learned

Successes and Wins - activities in which I have attempted new behavior successfully.

Date	Activity or Behavior and What I have learned

Challenges - activities remaining unfinished or presenting ongoing challenge for me

Date	Activity or Behavior and What I have learned

Challenges - activities remaining unfinished or presenting ongoing challenge for me

Date	Activity or Behavior and What I have learned

Challenges - activities remaining unfinished or presenting ongoing challenge for me

Date	Activity or Behavior and What I have learned

Challenges - activities remaining unfinished or presenting ongoing challenge for me

Date	Activity or Behavior and What I have learned

Action Plans - activities, assignments, projects or new approaches I should work on or complete to achieve my development goals.

Date	Action Step

Action Plans - activities, assignments, projects or new approaches I should work on or complete to achieve my development goals.

Date	Action Step

Action Plans - activities, assignments, projects or new approaches I should work on or complete to achieve my development goals.

Date	Action Step

Action Plans - activities, assignments, projects or new approaches I should work on or complete to achieve my development goals.

Date	Action Step

Information to Share with My Mentor
- issues I should discuss with my mentor, important new learning, or specific feedback I should give my mentor about our partnership, its progress or character.

Date	Topic

Information to Share with My Mentor

- issues I should discuss with my mentor, important new learning, or specific feedback I should give my mentor about our partnership, its progress or character.

Date	Topic

Information to Share with My Mentor

- issues I should discuss with my mentor, important new learning, or specific feedback I should give my mentor about our partnership, its progress or character.

Date	Topic

Information to Share with My Mentor

- issues I should discuss with my mentor, important new learning, or specific feedback I should give my mentor about our partnership, its progress or character.

Date	Topic

Conclusion

"There has been a calculated risk in every stage of American development - the pioneers who were not afraid of the wilderness, businessmen who were not afraid of failure, dreamers who were not afraid of action."

- Brooks Atkinson

Though it's likely you have used others as mentors - most of us have - it's less likely that you and a mentor have taken the intentional steps described in *The Mentee's Navigator*. It is our hope that this book continues to serve as a reference guide while you move through this and future mentoring years. We suggest that you refer to it often, checking on your growth goals, reassessing your mentee competencies and continually upgrading the quality of your mentoring partnerships.

We strongly advise that you regularly revisit and update the worksheets in the book. This is a great way to keep your learning antenna extended. The progress review sheets are also the place to capture your learning and insight before the lessons are lost or become fuzzy over time.

It is our hope that mentoring leads to your capturing some powerful insights about learning on the job, and that you will continue to apply these lessons throughout your career. In fact, we urge you to reflect seriously on what you have learned about learning on the job. As a final step, review the questions below to determine what you have discovered about focusing on professional growth while, at the same time, carrying out your regular responsibilities.

1. What insights have you gained about how you learn best?

2. What type of work assignments or projects produced the most learning and growth?

3. What is one aspect of your development during this mentoring period that you want to continue cultivating over the next six months?

4. What has been the most significant challenge you have faced while seeking to get the most from this mentoring opportunity?

5. What do you now know to be true about yourself as a learner that you may not have known before?

6. What would you do differently if you had the opportunity to work with a mentor again?

7. What did you learn during this experience that would assist you in mentoring someone else?

Appendix

ADDITIONAL FOCUS EXERCISES

FINDING A MENTOR

Appendix 1:
Additional Focus Exercises

The following exercises are offered as additional thinking aids in contemplating your mentoring goals and desired relationship with a mentor. They may prove helpful as you prepare for your initial Link-Up with a mentor or in preparing ideas for Renewal or redirection.

Exercise 1: Benefits you seek

Why do people want mentors? Below are some reasons they often give. Note the benefits below that are important to you. In the **Priority Check** column, identify your 5 highest priority reasons for working with a mentor.

What I want from a mentor	Priority Check
Shortcuts; how things really get done.	
Targeting a specific development need.	
Networking assistance and opportunities	
Getting advice without an agenda	
Learning more about myself	
Expanding my knowledge about the organization	
Helping me deal with issues or behaviors that I might resist confronting.	
Looking at things in ways that may be uncomfortable, or at least unfamiliar.	
Seeing how I can do more to affect my future.	
Getting help seeing the big picture.	
Having a partner, or friend to talk to in confidence about a whole variety of things.	
Getting the best results from my time and effort.	
Getting help in achieving developmental goals	
Getting hints on how my mentor has approached things.	
Expanding my talents and leadership capabilities.	

Exercise 2: **Your Professional Development Vision:** Describe your desired work situation 2 to 3 years from now:

The work I want to be doing involves:

_____
_____
_____
_____

In doing this work, I will be making the following contribution:

_____
_____
_____
_____

As a result of doing this work, I will have gained:

_____
_____
_____
_____

The knowledge I will need to have for this work is:

_____
_____
_____
_____

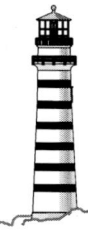

The ideal skills for this work (check all that apply)

X	Personal Skills	X	People Skills
	Managing priorities		Managing conflict
	Developing self-organization		Managing differences
	Practicing assertiveness		Listening
	Asking for what I want		Building strong relationships
	Building self-awareness of personal style		Demonstrating value for others
			Dealing with ambiguity
	Delivering on commitments		Taking calculated risks
X	Professional Skills	X	Leadership Skills
	Strategic thinking		Leading change
	Long-range planning		Managing change
	Building customer relationships		Building a team
	Excelling at customer service		Delegating
	Building technical skills		Coaching others
	Business writing		Empowering others
	Solving problems		Giving effective presentations
	Making decisions		Being approachable
	Acquiring business knowledge		

Exercise 3: Support that you seek

Your mentor will have some ideas about how to best support you. Keep in mind that only part of a mentor's role is to advise you. Mentors can lend support in a variety of ways: observing you in action and then providing their insight and impressions, creating assignments or projects to try, or exploring your patterns of thinking and responding to situations.

What kind of supports and learning experiences could a mentor help provide that would be of most benefit to you at this point? What kinds of assignments, if any, would provide these experiences?

Random Menu of Options
Install a new system
Integrate systems across units
Present a proposal to top management
Write up a policy statement
Run a task force on a business problem
Serve on a new product/project review committee
Study customer needs
Interview outsiders on views of the organization
Complete a project with a tight deadline
Write a proposal for a new trend/technique; present to others
Design a training course
Manage an ad hoc group of inexperienced people
Study history/draw business parallels
Take on an 'undoable' project (last person failed)
Become active in a professional organization
Mentor a younger or less experienced person
List other options below:

Appendix 2:
Finding a Mentor

Knowing the right steps to take early on can get a mentoring relationship moving in the right direction.

Know what you want and what you need.

One of the very first things you need to deal with is what type of mentoring relationship interests you. For example, you may want a mentor who is a senior leader very steeped in the business. Or maybe you would like your mentor to be someone closer to you in experience, but whom you feel could help you in specific areas of growth and knowledge.

Understanding what you most want from a mentor and what you yourself have to offer will help you decide what you want. What are your short-term goals - one or two years into the future? What knowledge, skills and abilities should you develop to meet these goals? Do you want knowledge and skills specific to your job? Marketing? Finance? Business structure? Operations and production? Or would you use a mentor for more generalized or abstract aims, like leadership methods, personal style, understanding and dealing with organizational politics, interpersonal effectiveness, or conflict resolution? Making yourself aware of your specific desires and needs will go a long way in deciding whom you should seek as a mentor.

Think about the characteristics of your "perfect mentor", the things you would like to learn, and how your mentor learned them. In your mind, take yourself into the future - for example, one year from now, and ask yourself what key experiences a mentor could provide that would be of most benefit to you. One of your biggest roles as a mentee is to become highly influential in getting the right mentor and making sure you are getting the help that most benefits you. Remember, you must be the "driver" and the "helmsman."

Select a mentor.
Knowing what kind of person would be best for you, it is time to look around. The best mentors are people who are excited about learning and who are continuing their own development. When choosing a mentor, look for people like that - people who are curious and are seeking self-improvement - they will be excited about helping someone else to grow, and that's what you want. The best mentors are those who get a sense of personal satisfaction from seeing others succeed. Good mentors have a desire to be active participants in others' learning and growth.

If no potential mentors come readily to mind, you can ask peers or managers if they know of any potential mentors for you or have heard about anyone who has expressed interest in being someone's mentor. Your organization may even have a mentoring program that can pair you with a mentor based on your goals and the mentor's knowledge and skills. Of course, you don't have to find a mentor within your organization. Attending meetings and events hosted by your professional association, social, education or religious group is an excellent way to meet a potential mentor.

Sometimes persistence is necessary. Several years ago, Tom, a colleague of ours wanted as his mentor a certain high ranking, gruff executive in his firm. The first time he asked him he got a very curt "No". He went back again, "No." And again, "No". The fourth time, the man said, gruffly, "Okay". Tom realized that the mentor wanted to be sure that he really had the fortitude to persevere, because that's the kind of protégé he wanted. That executive is still Tom's mentor today, years later.

Make a request.
Just as Tom did, once you've found someone you want as a mentor you'll need to approach that individual and ask. You will want to share what mentoring means to you and find out what your potential mentor perceives it to mean. If the person indicates an interest, arrange a time when you both can share your views and discuss a potential mentoring partnership. Having done your homework will be very beneficial at this point: share your short-term goals, your accomplishments and your major developmental needs and objectives. Let your potential mentor know what special areas you would like to concentrate on and connect all of these points to the reasons you are requesting him or her to be a mentor for you.

Be completely honest in your explanation why you want a mentor and why you are asking this particular individual. Don't be surprised by the reaction. Once the person hears your needs and objectives, he or she may tell you that they do not think they can help, or do not really want to take on the responsibility. Many who are asked to be mentors are honored at the request, and although they may not have considered mentoring someone before, often agree to give it a go. If the person agrees to begin a mentoring relationship, you'll want to have a focused conversation about what you both want to accomplish.

Prepare for the first meeting.
One of the objectives of your first meeting should be to establish goals for the mentoring relationship. Prepare for this meeting by considering the following questions:
- What should your mentor know about you in order to work most successfully with you?
- How do you learn best? By reading? Observing? Doing? Listening? Experimenting?
- What are your desired outcomes for the mentoring relationship?
- What do you expect from your mentor?
- How will you know when the relationship is working?

Before your first formal meeting, ask your mentor to come prepared with answers to questions such as: What do you expect from me as your mentee? What do you feel most able to help me with? How do you like to work with people you are teaching and developing? What are you looking for from having a mentoring relationship with a mentee? What do you see yourself gaining from this? A discussion about what you both wish to accomplish and gain will give your relationship direction. Also during the first meeting, decide on how often you will meet and whether you will communicate in person or via e-mail or telephone. Make sure you emphasize that you hope that scheduled meetings will not be the only time you communicate with each other. Before your meeting is over, decide on when you will meet next.

When you both have agreed to go forth with the mentoring relationship, you'll need to talk to your manager. After all, your manager is the one who has the functional responsibility for your performance and development. Let your manager know what role your mentor will play and ask for some guidance and support.

Your first two or three meetings should have some sort of structure to them. Discuss a question that you can work on prior to the next meeting. Prepare an answer for the next time you meet--this will give you something to structure the meeting around.

Finally, build in a feedback expectation into the relationship so both you and your mentor can say whether you are getting what you need out of the arrangement. This self-renewal capability can get your relationship back on track if it starts heading in the wrong direction.

Other Mentoring Products By Perrone-Ambrose Associates

A Mentor's Companion by Larry Ambrose, a managing partner of Perrone-Ambrose Associates, offers a journey through the mentoring interaction. It is a combination of behavioral menus and live dialogues between "high tech VP Ruth Merlin" and her mentee, "Manager Art Regent."

The Mentoring Field Guide collects the action checklists from A Mentor's Companion and puts them in an easy-to-find-and-use format. It will simplify the preparation for mentoring meetings with mentees and will improve Mentoring skills by making the use of best practices more consistent.

The Mentors 2100 Audit is a 360° feedback tool which measures critical skills in the six key areas of supporting, challenging, pathfinding, empowering, double-loop learning and managed learning. It lets the individual know how he/she actually behaves as a mentor and coach. Each Audit packet includes: 1 self assessment audit, 1 supervisor audit, 10 direct report/other audits, easy to use instructions, and a Results and Analysis Manual presented in a comprehensive easy-to-read format.

The Mentor Self-Assessment allows mentors to reflect upon their mentoring behavior and skill and to develop a plan for self-improvement. The Self-Assessment evaluates the same critical skill areas as the Mentors 2100 Audit in a do-it-yourself format. The assessment can be used as part of mentor skills training or as a stand-alone too.

The Mentee Self-Assessment is a self-scoring evaluation intended to assist in the knowledge and development of the individual on six competencies critical to a successful mentoring relationship. Employees will learn how they can be better mentees by examining their ratings on receptivity, self management, self-awareness, growth orientation, resilience and double-loop learning focus.

The Mentoring Compass is a 6" x 8" card that provides mentors with a directional approach in conducting the mentoring session. The reverse side lists questions and statements to assist the mentor.

The Mentors 2100 Series Pocket Prompter is a triple fold pocket-sized card for use when mentoring takes place away from one's desk. It lists competencies, questions, hints and reminders.

The Mentoring Guidelines Bookmark is a 3" x 8" laminate which states in "commandment" format the practices of a highly effective mentor.

Consulting Services
By
Perrone-Ambrose Associates

Perrone-Ambrose Associates, Inc., Was founded as an organization development firm in 1973. For nearly 20 of those years PAA has been perfecting and applying the concept of Mentoring in the Workplace as a key element of its total consultation practice.

Organizations across the country have sought the consulting experience of PAA for such endeavors as:

- Mentoring Systems Planning
- Mentor Skill Development
- Mentee Skill Development
- Coaching Skills for Managers
- Executive Coaching
- Coaching Skills for the Human Resource Professional
- Management Training
- Team Building

Notes

Notes

Notes